TABLE OF CONTENTS

Introduction

Explainer Video Basics
    Is an Explainer Video Right for You?
    The Psychology
    Case Studies

Explainer Video Styles and Uses
    Video Styles
    Verticals and Use Cases

Hiring and Working with an Explainer Video Production Company
    Hiring the Right Company for You
    The Typical Production Process
    Should You Write the Script?
    DIY Tools for Bootstrappers and Freelancers

Ways to Use Your Video
    Sales Teams
    Training and Internal Communication
    Trade Shows
    Raising Money
    Launching Products
    Digital Marketing
    Getting the Video onto Your Site

Conclusion

About the authors

Appendix A – Explainer Video Stats Infographic
Appendix B – Explainer Video Production Process Infographic
Appendix C – Script Example
Appendix D – Storyboard Example
Appendix F – Rypple Case Study
Appendix G – Dropbox Blog Post
Appendix F – Jellyfish Blog Post

INTRODUCTION

Video stats

700
videos are shared every minute on Twitter

100
hours of video are uploaded to YouTube in the same amount of time

source: YouTube.com

We live in an "information at hand," tech-driven world, with access to global knowledge available at our fingertips, 24 hours a day 7 days a week. Anything you ever wanted to know is literally waiting to be discovered on the internet.

Around the beginning of this shift in information sharing, the explainer video was created. First came Powerpoint, the grandfather of explainer videos. Images were combined with text to pitch or explain a product, service, program, or anything else.

With the advancement of technology, this form of packaged information evolved into explainer videos with moving graphics, characters, and an audio component. Now, viewers are more engaged than ever before.

EXPLAINER VIDEO BASICS

Is an Explainer Video Right for You?

YouTube stats

More than
1 billion
unique users visit YouTube each month

Over
6 billion
hours of video are watched each month on YouTube — that's almost an hour for every person on Earth, and 50% more than last year.

According to Nielsen, YouTube reaches more US adults ages 18-34 than any cable network

source: YouTube.com, September 2013

In 2007, the company Common Craft created an explainer video called Twitter in Plain English. The videos' objective was for its audience to understand exactly what Twitter was and how it functioned. They used simple graphics and straightforward wording to tell their story. The video was a success, and has gone on to generate almost 10 million views. Its creation marked the start of the explainer video era with an exclamation point.

Explainer videos provide help to any company looking to grow and build a strong customer base. It explains who you are or what you do and promotes your business at the same time. It's an excellent way to reach the audience you already have, and it's an even better way for new customers to discover you.

With the amount of time people spend on YouTube each month (over 6 billion hours watched), it's clear that video is a really important form of communication and it's here to stay. Everything and everyone is online, and an explainer video is a way to be included in the ever-growing online community.

There's no denying it, explainer videos are an investment in your company's future. With more and more people watching online videos, your investment will help you reach customers through one of the most attractive mediums available, a tool to attract customers for the next two to five years.

A video on Crazy Egg's homepage increased conversions by
64%

Source: CrazyEgg.com

Explainer videos are becoming a more important component of every company's marketing checklist. They've proven to generate leads, boost conversions, and increase sales while clearly explaining who you are and what you do. Are you ready to join the ranks of businesses investing in their future by making an explainer a part of your marketing mix?

The Psychology

There's a term we use here at Switch Video called Brain Science. Brain Science is essentially the psychology of audio and visuals working together in a single message. Our research has found that on average there is a 75% increase of understanding and application of the material when both auditory and visual senses are stimulated compared to just auditory. This means that the most effective way to get your message across is through video. Simply put, our brains are hardwired to respond to video messages. Three things to keep in mind:

The brain science of explainer videos

When stimulating only the auditory sense, on average people understand and can apply

47%

of the material presented vs

82%

when both auditory and visual senses are engaged

Simple Stories Sell – Our working memory can only handle so much information at one time. Overwhelming people with too many details leads to confusion, and confusing presentations are quickly forgotten. That's one reason why simple, concise explanations work better at getting your message across. The brain can only focus on and retain bite-sized bits of information throughout the viewing process.

Memories Matter – While the brain's working memory is rather limited, prior knowledge and stored memories influence a viewer's ability to understand content presented in your video. Explainer videos rely on metaphors to build on a viewer's past experience and knowledge. Relating products and services to things consumers already know goes a long way in building understanding and confidence in your company.

Video and Sound Create a Winning Team – Audio and video deliver a one-two punch that creates a lasting impression on the human brain. Research shows that, on average, people experience 75% greater understanding of the information delivered when using a combination of sight and sound. Studies also show that people retain 58% more information when both auditory and visual senses are stimulated.

Case Studies

Case Study #1: Rypple (now Work.com)

Work.com (formally Rypple before being aquired by Salesforce.com) wanted a video that would improve conversion rates on their website and engage visitors in a unique way.

Rypple placed the video on their home and landing pages, and tested it against a control page and another landing page containing a live action testimonial from Facebook.

Not only did Switch Video's landing page perform better, increasing conversions by 20%, but it also lowered the customer acquisition cost and generated leads that were more engaged and ready to use the product.

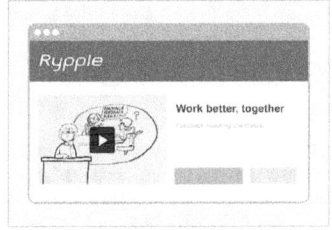

The Ripple video produced by Switch Video recorded a play rate of 30%, which is a 78% increase from the average play-rate for online videos. Not only so, but 56% of viewers traditionally watch half of an average two-minute video and only 40% of viewers watch the video through to completion. The Ripple video performed much better. 75% of viewers watched half of the video (an increase of 34%), and 50% watched the video through to completion (an increase of 25%).

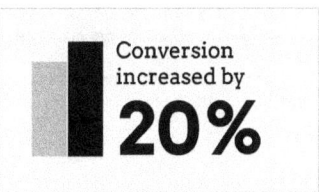

Jesse Goldman, VP of Customer Success at Ripple, had this to say about their video: "The video does a great job at explaining the problem Ripple solves, more than you can do in a small number of words on the page." And right he was because 1.8 million words is the equivalent of one minute of video, according to James McQuivey of Forrester.

Case study #2: Dropbox (produced by Common Craft)

Consumers who watch product videos are

85%

more likely to buy products, compared to those who do not watch product videos

Source: TMG; We Capture

In 5 years, Dropbox went from 0 to 100 Million users, all thanks to savvy marketing and an explainer video on their homepage. Dropbox's simple homepage design focused 100% of their visitors' attention on the explainer video.

There weren't any other links or messages that got in the way. The explainer video led to a 10% increase in conversions, and with 100 million users, that's 10 million extra customers from using an explainer video. With $4.80 of revenue per customer (based on estimates from 2011), that's an extra $48,000,000 in revenue per year.

EXPLAINER VIDEO STYLES AND USES

Styles

Whiteboard

Whiteboard is a very popular style because viewers are drawn in by a simple story unfolding as it's "drawn" before their eyes. It's engaging and fun to watch. Whiteboard videos tend to be the most professional and are great for businesses who speak to a more educated audience. This style contains images drawn by a digitized hand to appear as if you were drawing an explanation live in front of a group of people.

Client: IBM

2D

Two-dimensional graphics are another popular form of animation because of the creative options that come along with this style. They feature full color and animation that really bring your video to life. 2D animation is great for speaking to consumers and more general audiences. If you're looking for some extra creative whimsy to help your business or product stand out, 2D animation is the way to go!

Client: Juice Mobile

3D

Much like 2D, the creative possibilities are endless with the 3D style. The scenes are more polished and realistic. 3D videos, however, are exponentially more expensive than 2D animation due to the time and equipment that's required. 3D videos also aren't as simple as other styles and can overwhelm the viewers working memory. If you're looking to clearly communicate your message and make sure customers remember the most of what they watch, another style might be better.

Client: Nanagians

nanigans

Claymation

With claymation, characters and props are made out of clay or other materials, photographed frame by frame, and then edited together. This process is referred to as stop motion animation. They're highly creative, but come with a higher price tag due to the amount of time and work that goes into a claymation project. If you want something truly unique and impressive, and time is not of the essence, claymation may just be the style for you!

Client: Study Hall

Live Action

Live action uses real people, scenes, props, i.e. the whole works. This style is the real deal, literally. It's popular for commercials and movies and is offered by some explainer video companies. Live action is a great style, but it puts limitations on what you can do, unless you have a Hollywood budget. This style is better suited for promotional type of videos that have little explanation or education. Also, keep in mind that, at a certain point, the video will look dated since hairstyles, clothes, and film quality all go out of style.

Produced by:
Dollar Shave Club

Hybrid

That's right. Such a thing exists. Can't decide if you want stop motion or 2D animation? Mash them up like potatoes! It's possible to combine video styles; you just have to make sure it isn't distracting. The end result should be simple and clean, but you can combine whiteboarding with 2D animation or live action with 2D animation. It's totally up to you! Just ask the company you decide to go with about this option. They might not think to mention it, but it's completely doable. A hybrid style of video is always unique, and keeps the audience interested because of the

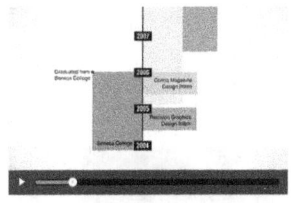

Client: Visualize.me   vizualize.me

Looking for Inspiration?

www.switchvideo.tv/dropbox/
Produced by Common Craft

1. What Is Dropbox?
Dropbox's original paper cut-out video used a story and metaphors to explain cloud computing before the concept was widely understood.

www.switchvideo.tv/coca-cola/
Produced by Cognitive Media

2. Coca-Cola Content 2020
Coca-Cola created a 7:57 whiteboard video to share their new brand strategy that revolves around content creation.

www.switchvideo.tv/dollarshaveclub
Produced by Dollar Shave Club

3. Dollar Shave Club
The Dollar Shave Club video uses humor and shock to connect with a universal experience and create a message that every guy can relate to.

www.switchvideo.tv/mailbox
Produced by Mailbox

4. Mailbox
The live action video MailBox created to introduce their app used imagery, live action, text, and music to tell a story without words that was both descriptive as well as inspiration.

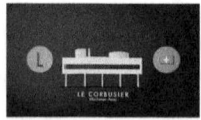
www.switchvideo.tv/abc
Produced by Andrea Stinga and Federico Gonzalez

5. The ABC of Architects
Andrea Stinga and Federico Gonzalez created a motion graphic video as a shareable piece of content that presents the top architects listed A to Z along with their best known building.

For more inspriration, check out our list of the best explainer videos at
http://www.switchvideo.com/resources/the-best-explainer-videos/

Verticals and Use Cases

While explainer videos are typically used to explain complex ideas or content, they have different use cases depending on the vertical.

Whether you're a technology company, a pharmaceutical company, or a non-profit, there's a style and use case that will work for you. We've had the privilege of working in many different verticals. Below is a list of ways explainer videos can be used based on the industry in question, but this is by no means an exhaustive list. As you read through, consider the many different ways you can use an explainer video for your business.

Automotive
Product performance
Industry statistics
Car features
Parts description

Bio-Tech
Product background
Patient education
Product instructions

Consumer and Packaged Goods
Advertisement
Product story
Sales tool for email
Social media contest explainer

Education
Campaign education
Public education
Employee education/training
Mentorship

Finance
Education tool about financial matters
Billing update
Policy shift announcement
Financial tool description

Food and Beverage
Public relations campaign
Advertisement

Fundraising and Advocacy
Campaign video
Educational video with sponsor mention
Contributor recognition/thank you

Government
Policy education
Instructional/process
Compliance education

Health and Beauty
Product feature
Social media contest
Tips and tricks

Human Resources
Compliance and code of conduct
Employee training
Internal messaging and procedure
Internal announcements

Industrial
Technology education
Machine training
Certification standards

Insurance
Public education
Policy review

Manufacturing
Channel partner communication
Channel standards
Sourcing information

Marketing
Product orientation
Brand positioning
Sales and outreach tools

Medical + Pharmaceutical
Patient education
Epidemiology education
Public education
Physician education

Professional Services
Compliance certification
Value proposition
Trade show booth

Real Estate
Financing information
Insurance regulations
Property developer promotion

Retail
Product offering
Order process orientation

Shipping and Logistics
Shipping chain education
Distributor information
General promotions

Social Media
Contest regulations
Customer education
Campaign education

Tech/Software
Product explainer
Data visualization
Demo

Telecommunications
Billing explainer
Product/package information
Network explainer

Tourism and Hospitality
Promotional
Training
Compliance and regulatory

HIRING AND WORKING WITH AN EXPLAINER VIDEO PRODUCTION COMPANY

Hiring the Right Company for You

The first thing to do is research, watch explainer videos from different companies and find out what their process is. Make sure you gather an adequate amount of information on the topic so when you go to make a decision, it's one you feel good about. There's no right or wrong answer across the board, but there is a right or wrong answer for you. Make sure you don't feel bullied or pressed. If you do, that's not a good company to work with. You are the client commissioning the product, so make sure the company you work with is happy to work with you and is one you'll get along with.

A good place to begin is a company's portfolio. What clients have they worked with? Do they have a lot of experience? A portfolio lays it all out on the line and gives you the best idea about what your video will look like.

Enjoying who you work with is a key part of the video production process because how much you enjoy the process will show in the final product.

Going with a company you feel good about eliminates the onset of potential headaches along the way. If you get frustrated with the company when discussing the project, it's only going to get harder once you start making a video. You want to have fun making your explainer video! This is really important because it will come across in the finished product.

The Typical Production Process

We have a proven, 5-step process we follow here at Switch Video to consistently make effective explainer videos. The details vary at different explainer video production houses, but the process is fairly the same across the board. Here is a step-by-step overview of what our production process is like.

Step 1 : Discovery

This step sometimes gets skipped with other companies, but we make sure to always start with a proper discovery phase. Discovery is where we go over the details of the project, our process, how we do things and find out what the client is looking for. This is vital to making sure we deliver exactly what the client wants and sets a flow for the duration of the project.

Step 2 : Script

Higher end companies will have a professional writer on staff to write the script for you. In-house script writers will usually have direct contact with clients whereas outsourced writers will not. The scriptwriter will send clients multiple concepts for their review, based on what they were looking for in the discovery part of the process. They will make edits and adjustments according to what the clients' specifications are. When all is approved the script moves into the storyboard phase.

Step 3: Storyboard

A professional begins the storyboard phase once the client has a general idea of what they want for visuals. A storyboard shows still images next to a script, providing the client with a clearer idea of what the final product will look like.

Step 4: Animation

This is where the animator puts everything into motion! At this point the storyboard has been approved by the client and now it's time to animate the characters and images. Again, just like a scriptwriter, a good animator will work in-house and can be contacted by the client directly. During the discovery portion of the project, we conduct a call with the client and all members of the team working on that project present and in the same room. A good way to tell if your video team all works together in the same office is if they're on calls together. Otherwise, your video may be getting outsourced.

Step 5: Delivery

Your project is complete! Your explainer video is ready to share with your potential customers in any number of ways. Your video producer will provide you with a number of different file formats, will help you with video storage, and will show you how to embed your video on your website and into emails.

Should You Write the Script?

There's a slight debate over whether or not you should write your own script or have an agency write it for you. Neil Patel, for one, says that you should write it yourself. Here's our take on the subject:

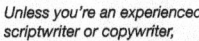

Unless you're an experienced scriptwriter or copywriter,

You shouldn't write it yourself

It's hard work. At Switch it took us producing 200 videos before we got really good at what we do.

If you can take advantage of a full service production company, then you should. Neil is right that you know your product the best. He's also right that you should interview your past clients and website visitors and use their comments to help you inform the scriptwriter.

The best approach is to share your knowledge with the experts you've hired through a guided briefing process so that your ideas are tested by the experts. If anything, you need to let the production house push back against your ideas. That's the feedback we received a few years ago. A lot of our clients wanted us to stop listening to them so much. Why? Because they wanted a better video, not a company that says yes to whatever they asked for.

When you write your own script, you don't get the outside perspective from someone who's not dealing with your product day in and day out. If you're a marketing genius, you may be able to pull it off, like Neil Patel, but if not, having someone provide another perspective is what will take your script from good to great. When we produced our videos here at Switch recently, Andrew, our founder, shared his goals for the video, and then let the team work their magic. He didn't want to get in the way. He felt too close to the project and that he needed the team to work on it without his interjections. The end result was a much better video.

Neil is right that the script is the key to producing an awesome video and that you should use your extensive product knowledge, client knowledge, and skills to contribute to the video production process when you're working with your production team.

If you want to get a head start on your own or if you just can't afford a full service company, visit the appendix to find scriptwriter tips, examples, and templates.

Tools for Bootstrappers

Want to make your own video? Here are some tools that can help you along the way:

SPARKOL®

GINGER

Sparkol VideoScribe allows you to create fast rendering, high-definition stop-motion capture videos. With a Pro account, you have full access to animation and music files, and you have the ability to use the videos commercially without any watermark.

Ginger lets you create simple videos with ease through a two-step process. You record your voice work, and their system automatically matches your project up with relevant graphics. After just a bit of tweaking, your explainer video is ready to deliver.

Camtasia Studio®

Go!Animate

Using **Camtasia**, you can record what's happening on your computer screen. Afterward, use their powerful video design studio to add in the elements like animations, sounds, themes and backgrounds.

Tools like **GoAnimate!** and **PowToons** try to simplify the process further with drag-and-drop menus you can use to create your own animations.

WAYS TO USE YOUR VIDEO

As you may have noticed in previous sections, there are more ways to use your video than placing it on your website. You can use it for marketing, advertising, sales, training, and internal communications, depending on your goal for the project and the type of video you produce. Here's a list of several creative ways you can use your video.

Sales Teams

Have you realized your sales team can take advantage of your new video? You can share the video with your sales team members and have them send the video to prospective clients. We had one client who e-mailed a potential customer on LinkedIn in the first week after their video was made. They ended up closing an $800k deal, all from e-mailing a video to a cold lead. That's a powerful use for video and shows how much of a return you can get on your investment.

Training and Internal Communications

Another use for your video is training and internal communications. We've created these types of videos for HP, Home Depot, and Pearson Education to communicate new initiatives with the entire company. You can use a video to train employees or to explain changes within an organization such as an upcoming merger. Explainer videos are a great way to clearly communicate an important message to all of your employees.

Trade Shows

Do you have a trade show coming up? Have you thought about giving video a try? Working a trade show booth can really suck, but working a booth across from a competitor who has a video is the worst of all. Videos bring prospective customers to a booth like moths to a flame.

If you're at a booth without a video, people have to decide to talk to you before they stop by. They have to be ready to commit to talking to someone before slowing down and making their way over to your booth. It's different when you have a video. Prospects are compelled to stop and relax for a minute before they decide to engage in a conversation. This creates a normal, tranquil moment in the midst of a crazy trade show environment where people can take a break from high-pressure sales tactics. It creates a natural transition and an easy way to start a conversation.

Raising Money

Not only can you use your video for marketing and internal communications; you can also use it to raise money. Dropbox used an explainer video to impress venture capitalists as a way to get funding. You can also use an explainer video on a site like Kickstarter to generate funding. And Once you do have funding, you can create another video to communicate with your customers as a way to leverage the funding you received and to line up customers for your product.

Launching Products

Product launches are another great time to use explainer videos. Google used one to announce Google Drive once it became available, and many of our clients have used video in the same way. It's a great way to announce a new product and to make sure your customers know how it works.

Digital Marketing

Digital marketing is the number one way people use explainer videos. They put them on their site to increase conversion rates, and they advertise with them on sites like Youtube and LinkedIn. Hopefully by now you've learned that digital marketing isn't the only way to use your video, but it is a great way to use it.

Getting the Video onto Your Site

Last but not least, you need to figure out how to get the video onto your site. The good news is that there are quite a few hosting options available. You can use YouTube, Vimeo, Brightcove Video, Ooyala, Wistia, or VidYard. We use VidYard because they provide great analytics and also ensure that the video plays across desktop and mobile devices.

Our number one recommendation is not to host the video yourself. You might consider this for the sake of saving money, but it's not worth it. Self hosting is more work and effort than it needs to be, and you aren't guaranteed your video will play on all mobile devices. However, if you are budget conscious, YouTube is a great option because it's free and works across any device.

CONCLUSION

Hopefully, you've learned a lot about corporate explainer videos by reading this guide. Creating one and using it properly isn't necessarily rocket science, but it helps to learn as much as you can so you can get the best results possible with your video.

Explainer videos have proven to be great for businesses in every imaginable industry. Our clients range from pharmaceutical companies to software businesses to professional service providers, and all of them have found animated video as a great way to tell their story and to explain what they do.

Whether you're looking to increase conversion rates on your website or explain a change to employees within your organization, explainer videos are an excellent way to share your ideas in a format that people will watch and remember.

WHO IS SWITCH VIDEO?

We create animated explainer videos for companies like Facebook, IBM, HP, Bayer, Abbott, and many more. We've made 450+ videos for clients in 15 countries and 10 different languages. That's a lot of videos so it's good that we love what we do.

over
450
videos

clients from
15
countries

videos in
10
languages

Our goal with each new project is to unlock the full potential of every idea, product, or business we work on. Clients come to us with challenging new concepts every day, and we take pride in unleashing the full potential of each and every idea. Whether it's a product that's difficult to explain or a business that seems boring, we do what it takes to distill each concept into a simple message that's easy to understand and connects emotionally with customers. If you're looking to create an explainer video that tells your company's story and gets your customers to take action, we'd love to work together.

ABOUT THE AUTHORS

Andrew Angus

Andrew Angus is the founder and CEO of Switch Video. With over 450 videos produced since the start of Switch Video, Andrew's passion is to provide clients with exceptional service and a product they can be proud of.

Switch Video's animated explainer videos aren't just cute, funny and entertaining – they're proven effective marketing tools used by companies in 15 countries and in 10 different languages. Past clients include Microsoft, American Express, IBM, HP and many more.

Andrew led the movement to integrate brain science and web metrics into the production of animated explainer videos. He is a thought-leader in the online video industry, writing and speaking about how to produce simple videos that "explain what you do" in an engaging and compelling format. His book, 60 Seconds – How to tell your company's story and the brain science to make it stick, is available on Amazon. Andrew welcomes people to reach out to him on Twitter or Google+ and can be booked to speak on Speakerfile.

Heather McKibbon

Heather is a salty dog at heart, thriving anywhere near the coastline. Currently living in San Francisco and heading up the business development team at Switch, she brings a wealth of enthusiasm and a love for her clients. She has a BSc in Biology and International Development that she's put to good use working as a program director and professional fundraiser for organizations in the private and non-profit sector around the world.

Her current responsibilities here at Switch include taking an active role in developing the content marketing strategy and coordinating efforts to reach a larger audience.

In her spare time, Heather builds bonfires, hikes, explores the underwater world (usually when her kayak tips) and indulges in the baking arts where she has mastered the love of chocolate ganache.

Appendix A – Explainer Video Stats Infographic
http://www.switchvideo.com/research/explainer-video-infographic/

Appendix B – Explainer Video Production Process Infographic
http://www.switchvideo.com/company/process/

Appendix C – Script Example
http://www.switchvideo.com/example-script-storyboard

Appendix D – Storyboard Example
http://www.switchvideo.com/example-script-storyboard

Appendix F – Rypple Case Study
http://www.switchvideo.com/Rypple_Case_Study.pdf

Appendix G – Dropbox Blog Post
http://www.switchvideo.com/blog/2013/01/10/how-an-explainer-video-helped-dropbox-grow-from-0-to-100-million-users/

Appendix F - Jellyfish Blog Post
http://www.switchvideo.com/blog/2013/04/25/800k-deal-in-7-days-a-switch-video-success-story/

WANT TO LEARN MORE?

Check out more explainer video resources at www.switchvideo.com/research

60 Seconds
Learn about how to simplify your company's story so that people know what you do.

Rypple Case Study
The Rypple case study demonstrates the power of the explainer video, which showed an increase of 20% on home page conversions.

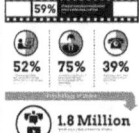

Video Marketing Infographic
Why video is so effective and what the results are.

www.ingramcontent.com/pod-product-compliance
Lightning Source LLC
Chambersburg PA
CBHW051830170526
45167CB00005B/2226